WOMEN OF GOD,
Arise!

Books by

TERESA SMYSER

FICTION
Contemporary Romance

Heaven Help Us!

Historical Romance
The Warrior Bride Series

The Warrior & Lady Rebel

In His Embrace

Capture a Heart of Stone

WOMEN OF GOD,
Arise!

CONQUER DAILY GOLIATHS
WITH GODLY POWER!

TERESA SMYSER

Teresa Smyser
Jer 29:11

To my sweet granddaughters,
Emery & Thea.
May you grow to be women of God!

Contents

ACKNOWLEDGMENTS

As with any book, it takes a tribe of people to help bring it to completion. This one is no exception. I spent hours listening to sermons and reading books by Charles Stanley, David Jeremiah, Francis Chan, Tony Evans, and my own dynamic pastor, Joel Carwile. These men know how to preach the Word and offer biblical truths with an easy understanding. Their tutoring allowed me to write with confidence as I interpreted the scriptures.

After each chapter is completed, I place it in the proficient hands of my editor, Joan Orman. She treats my manuscript with dignity even as her red pen slashes through my mistakes. I appreciate each of her comments as we work together to present a quality book for my readers.

No author is complete without her beta readers. Thank you Whiney Kroh, Lynn Brown, Sandi Donaldson, Lauren Cox, and Jo Lena Corkern. I know you love me enough to tell the truth about my rough drafts. I truly appreciate each suggestion for improvement.

When my manuscript nears completion, I turn to my gifted graphic designer, Whitley Fleming. She has such a talent in capturing the essence of my book with a spectacular cover. I'm grateful God placed her in my path.

Then there is my best friend who happens to be my sweet husband, Keith. He endures as I complain about the difficulty of writing my first non-fiction book for women. I'm sure he rolled his eyes more than a few times at my grumblings; yet he has stuck by my side for over forty years. Thank you for encouraging me, being a spiritual consultant, and loving me through this arduous process.

Above all else, honor to my Lord and Savior, Jesus Christ. To Him be the glory! Great things He has done!

Introduction

In the midst of prevailing evil surrounding us, women embrace words of wisdom that help them navigate through their fallen worlds. This book offers encouragement, hope, and the practical artillery needed to stand firm in a world spiraling deeper into spiritual darkness.

As our world continues to crumble under the onslaught of evil, each crisis women encounter has the power either to draw them closer to God or push them farther from Him. Women can survive and emerge victorious by working through their trials when they are equipped with the right defense.

Our society has fallen away from God's guidelines and needs to be drawn back to the basics of Godly principles. In this book we will unlock key elements for achieving victories over daily battles.

These segments are in no way the totality of all the Bible offers in the way of fighting our enemy; but the ones I have chosen, once implemented in your life, will help you make a difference in the moral climate in your home, your community, and our nation.

I am overjoyed that you have chosen to take this journey with me. However, before we place our feet on the path, we must suit up for battle. You can count on Satan's attacks when you pursue God's standards for living. To be victorious in this spiritual warfare against Satan and his demons, you need to put on the full armor of God found in Ephesians 6:14-17. Here we read about five components of defensive armor with one offensive weapon with which to do battle.

. . . Gird yourself with truth . . . The Roman soldier wore a loose-fitting tunic that could potentially hinder him in battle. Therefore, he used a belt to cinch up the excessive material. For us *truthfulness* is the belt that pulls all of our spiritual loose ends together. Satan fights with lies, and sometimes his lies sound like the truth. But do not fear; believers have God's truth for a counterattack which can defeat the devil's lies.

. . . Put on the breastplate of righteousness . . . The breastplate was a sleeveless piece of leather covering the soldier's full torso protecting the heart and vital organs. Since the heart is the seat of our emotions—self-worth and trust—we need to guard our hearts. This protection will come from *righteousness* which is a distinct characteristic of God Himself. As Christians walk in faithful

obedience to Christ Jesus, His righteousness will produce a spiritual breastplate for our defense.

*. . . **Stand firm in the gospel of peace** . . .* Roman soldiers wore boots with nails in them to grip the ground when in combat. When we talk about the gospel of peace, it pertains to the good news that believers can be at peace with God as we share His gospel. Satan says sharing God's Word is a worthless and hopeless task. Not true! We have the news everyone needs to hear even though some flounder around unaware of what they lack. So we must spread the gospel of peace knowing that God is fighting for us so that we can stand firm in His strength.

*. . . **Shield your body with faith** . . .* The soldier also carried a large shield that protected the entire body. It was an oil-treated leather shield. Our strong shield is one of faith. We need to have a basic trust in God's Word and His promises to guard us against Satan's lies and promises of pleasure. Deflect Satan's flaming arrows of temptation with obedience to God. See beyond your circumstances and know that the ultimate victory is yours!

*. . . **The helmet of Salvation** . . .* The helmet protected the soldier's head—a major target in battle. Put on your helmet of salvation to protect your mind from doubt and discouragement. Satan is delighted when we doubt that God is actually in charge of all happenings in our lives. He will seek to destroy all believers' assurance of salvation with his arsenal. Be safeguarded. Be prepared. Wear the helmet!

*. . . **The sword of the Spirit** . . .* The short sword was the soldier's only weapon to use offensively. Our sword is not made of metal or steel, but is the Word of God *"that is sharper than any two-edged blade."* Hebrews 4:12. There are times when we don't need to wait for evil to attack but take an offensive stance against it.

Put on each piece of armor with prayer so that you can draw from God's divine resources. Therefore, take up your sword to overpower all of Satan's strategies against you. God's Word is infinitely more powerful than any of Satan's weapons.

Now that you're suited up for battle, let's get started.

Chapter 1

Who's In Charge?

If you ever watch TV news, read a newspaper, or listen to a news radio, you realize that we live in a twisted world—wrong is right and right is wrong. Faced with making decisions based on half-truths, lies, and deception, how are we to survive, let alone thrive in such chaos? Girls, if we ever hope to navigate through this day-to-day jungle we call earth, we must get our priorities in order. So, settle into a comfy chair and get ready to receive practical ways you can stand firm and conquer your difficulties with Godly power.

Like you, I too have faced trials. Both of my newborn babies spent a week in NICU with life-threatening low platelet counts.

When I was twenty-six years old, my twenty-one-month old son had open-heart surgery. I stood by my husband as he underwent cancer surgery and treatments. My father died from heart failure. Any one of those devastating blows could have reduced me to mush. Instead, with each new hardship, God pulled me back from the precipice of despair and hopelessness. He reminded me to put Him first in my life and leave the consequences to Him. In Matthew 22:37-38 "Jesus said, *'You shall love the Lord your God with all your heart, with all your soul, and with all your mind.' This is the first and great commandment."*

From the beginning of time, God created us in His own image. No other part of God's creation can have the relationship to God as a man and a woman can possess. Our heavenly Father yearns for a loving relationship with you . . . yes, you . . . the broken and messed up . . . the lost and confused . . . the sinful and scarred woman. So journey with me as we unpack the scriptures to see how this close relationship can be attained in your life. If you don't know God intimately or are skeptical of His existence, then I urge you to read the back page where you will find His invitation to you. God can and will hear your voice when you seek Him with an honest heart. Even if you are unable to commit to trust Him today, please continue to read and see what God reveals to you. You will not be disappointed. Oh, you might want to have a Bible at your side. Don't own a Bible? No worries. I will include most scripture references in the body of the book or you can find them on the internet.

As you progress further into this book, you can expect Satan's attack. Satan has no desire for you to succeed as you seek God's direction. He likes to take your everyday occurrences and distort them to make you think the incidences are your enemies. A sick child, a grumpy husband, a disgruntled work associate, a hateful neighbor, busyness, or your own bad attitude—these may be the problems that threaten you. Don't let any of these arrows from Satan hinder you. Keep reading—you can be victorious with God's power!

God created you for the main purpose of a relationship with Him. Stop a moment and let that sink in. He loves you and wants to be with you every day. He knows the more time you spend with Him, the more you will look like Him—wise, virtuous, humble, patient, kind, giving, forgiving—to name a few. With that in mind, what does it mean to put God first in your life? Let's refer to Matthew 22:27 where we read *". . . Love the Lord your God with all your heart, with all your soul, and with all your mind."* Deep within us, we each want to be loved—the no-holds-barred kind of love. One way to foster this type of love is to spend time with people dear to our hearts.

I remember when my husband, Keith, and I decided we loved each other. It was the summer before Keith left for seminary, and I had started my sophomore year in college. He likes to remind me that he said those three little words to me first—always the competitor. Anyway, after we made that earth-shattering declaration, we attempted to spend every available moment together. We knew once he left for New Orleans Theological Seminary that 842 miles would separate us, and talking daily would not occur. For you young gals, the invention of cell phones was still in the future and long-distance phone calls were very expensive.

Prior to his departure, during the summer of 1976, if we weren't in each other's company physically, Keith and I talked on the phone daily. We longed to share our feelings, experiences, hurts, dreams, joys, and thoughts about the future. He was my knight in shining armor, and I was his lady. As a result, we longed to be together; and we consciously chose to spend time with one another.

> ## Spend time reading God's Word.

God desires closeness with you, too. He wants you to spend time with Him. One way to do that is by reading His Word. The Bible is like the ultimate play book for life. It contains standards for life issues you may face complete with examples of how to handle those problems. Do you spend time reading the Bible every day? If not, why not? I used to think I was too busy to read His

Word every day. But you know what I realized? I found time to do what I wanted. I can remember desperately trying to complete my children's photo albums. Photos, album pages, scissors, die cuts, and other Creative Memory items went with me in my car. As I waited in numerous car lines or at soccer practice, I worked on cutting and shaping pictures for those albums. Yes. I used my time wisely. It's a matter of being prepared when those quick moments appear. When I realized that my time with God was much more important than photo albums, I began to carry my Bible in the car or in my purse. You might want to consider this plan as well. Then when free time develops, you can use the time to learn more about Jesus. Fertilize that relationship and watch it blossom.

Psalm 119:162 says, *"I rejoice at Your word as one who finds great treasure."* Reading God's Holy Word is like a treasure hunt or feasting on a gourmet meal. You find wealthy nuggets of information that enrich your life beyond what you could imagine for yourself. The more knowledge and understanding you possess, the closer you draw to God. The closer you draw to God, the more you can experience His love and forgiveness—two things we all desire. The more you experience His love, the deeper you fall in love with Him. Do you see how this connection is building? Just like eating meal after meal to sustain your existence, developing a closeness with God is an ongoing process; but don't worry. No one has ever become sick or died from eating too much of God's Word. So chow down, girlfriend.

5

Meditate on God's Word.

Another way of putting God first is by meditating on His Word during the day. We all need to admit the truth. There are times during the day when our minds wander. It might be when we're sorting laundry, folding clothes, loading the dishwasher, vacuuming, taking a shower, driving to work, eating our lunch, or any number of other times. What better occasion to meditate on God's Word? You might choose to sing a praise chorus, to sing the scriptures, or simply to repeat verses you have memorized. To this day, the verses I remember easiest are the ones I put to music. When I make up a tune for the verse I'm working to memorize, it sticks with me. Not musical? No problem. Write your favorite verses on small index cards and carry them in your pocket. At home you might wish to tape them in strategic places. When I used to spend hours in my car, I taped mine on the steering wheel. Of course, I had to refrain from looking at the scripture card when turning a corner. Can you say *dizzy?*

In Psalm 119:97 we read, *"Oh, how I love Your law! It is my meditation all the day."* Intimate familiarity with God's law results in wise and discerning behavior. If you continue to read Psalm 119 verses 98-100, you find that believers who acquire wisdom from reading the Bible are wiser than those without God's Word. God blesses you with this wisdom, not to hold it over others, but to use it for His glory and to help guide you through this sinful world. True wisdom is applying knowledge in a life-changing way. With God's Word hidden in your heart, you can pull it up instantly when you need to fight Satan's attacks. Hiding God's Word in your heart is like a shield deflecting flaming arrows. 1 Peter 5:8 reads, *"Be sober, be vigilant; because your adversary the devil walks about like a roaring lion, seeking whom he may devour."* We live in a perpetual war zone. You must be ready!

> # God desires to hear from you.

It's a natural tendency to call your husband or a girlfriend when you want to share an exciting tidbit about your day. What if you have hurt feelings or the grumbles? *Talk, talk, talk, talk, talk.* You can't contain yourself. How about bending God's ear first? He cares for His people more than the rest of His creation. You are His sweet princess, and He wants to hear about your day and all that it encompasses. Therefore, nothing you encounter is too silly or outlandish for God to hear about it. You are safe to share your innermost thoughts and feelings. Have you ever disagreed with your husband? How are you to honor your husband's wishes when you can't agree? The best course of action is to take your problem to God. After crawling into God's lap, your conversation might sound something like this:

God, it's me again. Did you hear my husband's idea? Of course, You heard it. I personally think it's a harebrained idea, and I want You to fix it. Don't you think my idea is better? No? Maybe? He also hurt my feelings with his words. They were a bit harsh, don't You think? . . . You're right; maybe I'm overly sensitive right now. Either way, please change him . . . okay, or change me if that's what it takes to work out this argument. I'm leaving it with You. Thanks for listening. I love You, Lord. Amen.

Always take your frustration, hurts, anger and anxiety to the One who can fix the problem. As you pour out your pain to God, listen for His answer. He will use these times of intimacy to comfort and to teach you through them. Remember—nothing He allows into your life is wasted, not even pain. He has a reason for the pain even if you don't understand it.

Worry is a waste. Trust God.

Finally, in Matthew 6:33 we read, *"But seek first the kingdom of God and His righteousness, and all these things shall be added to you."* What things will be added to you? I'm glad you asked. Go ahead and read Matthew 6:25-34. I'll wait for you.

8

Ah, ha. God is speaking about worry. Let's talk about anxiety/worry for a moment. According to Webster worry is: *n.* "a state of anxiety and uncertainty over actual or potential problems. *v.* allow one's mind to dwell on difficulty or troubles; to tear at, gnaw on." Please note it says potential problems. You might have heard the saying that most things we worry about never come to fruition. What are some things you worry about? Your husband, children, health, finances, where you live, what people think of you, your body weight . . . the list can be endless. If you believe you are in charge of your life, your anxiety level increases when disaster strikes or you fail to meet demands or you fail to live up to expectations. Your heart races; your palms sweat; you're stressed out. Before you totally cave into the pressures of this world, remember what Peter said in 1Peter 5:6-7: *"Therefore humble yourselves under the mighty hand of God, that He may exalt you in due time, casting all your care upon Him, for He cares for you."*

In this scripture, casting is a deliberate act of setting something down and leaving it down. So dump those nasty problems at the feet of Jesus and leave them there. Don't buy into the thinking that if you're not worrying about the problem then you're not concerned. Hogwash! Ditch that idea and live worry free—almost. I say *almost* because I know there will be times when you feel the need to jerk your problems out of Jesus's hands and stuff them into your trusty backpack. You know the one . . . the heavy weight on your back . . . the one hurting your shoulders. The overstuffed bag where you cram worries that don't even belong to you—the prize possessions of friends and family. Whew! Ladies, we wear ourselves out with this line of action.

Believe me. I'm speaking to myself. In my past, I was a professional worrier. Since I like to manage events in my life, happenings out of my control throw me into a worry fest. One such ordeal—moving—proved traumatic for me. Each new position my husband accepted didn't just move us across town or even across the same state. The job change moved us out of the state in which we lived. The relocation gave me plenty of details to worry about. Where would we live? Would my children make friends? Would they like their new schools? Would I need to find employment? How many hours would it take to get home to our family in Kentucky? You get the idea. Needless to say, my bag of worries was bulging. I could easily pull numerous worries out of my bag and fret over them all at the same time. As I said, I was a professional. I'm here to tell you, it was wasted time; and it stole my joy in the process. Even though we moved to five different states and one state twice, God provided exactly what our family needed with every move.

> Irrational
> Illogical
> Ineffective

Girls, we can't afford to allow our circumstances to tear us apart. For a woman of God, worry is irrational, illogical, and ineffective. Regardless of your troubles, God has your best interests at heart and wants you to trust Him to care for you. We read in Matthew 6:32-33 where He promised to take care of our essential needs. Don't be a slow learner like me and worry away precious moments. As each day dawns, you must answer the question: Do I trust God to provide today or can I do a better job? You can't! The truth is that no matter how hard you try to control your circumstances, it's impossible!

News flash! God is in charge, not you. He's the Creator and you, the created. He can handle your life issues better than you. Surrender to His leadership today and face each challenge with the peace of knowing that Jesus is by your side through it all. As you draw closer to God, you can avail yourself of His strength and His hope. Matthew 11:28 says, *"Come to Me, all you who labor and are heavy laden. I will give you rest."* The word *come* means "Come now!" He invites those of us who are overworked, tension filled, or burned out from external pressures to rejuvenate in His presence. He never scolds us for being weak or foolish but promises to restore our weary souls like cold water to a parched throat—pure bliss!

In this first chapter, I wanted to stress the importance of giving God His rightful place in your life. Putting Him first is your number one priority. As we look back through these pages, I want you to remember the four practical ways to put God first.

- Read the Bible daily
- Meditate on His Word
- Talk to God through prayer
- Trust God by putting aside all worry

Choose at least one way of drawing closer to God and implement it this week. Remember, as you put God first each day, He will show you what to do; and He will take care of the consequences. Trust Him!

I leave you with my favorite Bible verse, Jeremiah 29:11, *"For I know the thoughts that I think toward you, says the Lord, thoughts of peace and not of evil, to give you a future and a hope."* With your foot on the path toward a victorious life, don't stop now; continue on to Chapter Two. I'll meet you there.

Before you turn this page, prayerfully consider where you want God to be in your life. Each day you must willfully decide who is going to be *in charge* and rule your heart—God or your own selfish self. If you have chosen God to be first in your life, then sign and date this page.

Date_____Signature_____

DIG DEEPER

Chapter 1

1. What arrow of discontent has Satan shot at you recently?

2. Name one Christ-like virtue you hope to nurture in your life.

3. Are you reading and applying God's playbook to your life? If not, why not?

4. What's a favorite scripture verse you've memorized? Why is it special to you?

5. Name a worry you want to release to God. Why are you holding onto it?

6. To draw closer to God, in what area do you need to improve?

Chapter 2

Do I Have to Obey?

I'm glad you made it a bit further down the path. Did you remember to put on your full armor of God? No? Every soldier needs protection, so prayerfully suit up by reading Ephesians 6:14-17 or the introduction. Sharpen your sword and oil up your shield to deflect Satan's arrows of defeat and doubt. We're headed deeper into the battle zone where obedience will be put to the test.

Hopefully, you agree that God needs to be the leader or commander of this war waged against Satan—the destroyer of our world. Now before you say it, I can hear what you're thinking. *"Wait a minute. Put on the brakes. I didn't sign up to read a book about waging war against Satan. I want my money back."* Hold tight. In Ephesians 6:12, we read: *"For we do not wrestle against flesh and blood, but against principalities, against powers, against the rulers of the darkness of this age, against spiritual hosts of wickedness in the heavenly places.* " Satan's war against God's people is an organized strategy. Like a military general, he's clever, crafty, and cunning. You may think it's people who betray or hurt you—no, my friend. The real battle is against Satan who brings evil into your life and tempts you to sin. Knowing this truth will help you vanquish the true foe.

Whew! For a moment, I thought I'd lost you. I'm glad you have put God first in your life and are willing to follow Him to the next step. With that in mind, let's talk about your part. Hand-in-hand with putting God first is obedience to His commands. Webster defines obedience this way: "the state or fact of being obedient; doing what is ordered; submission."

Confession time. In my family tree there is a long line of stubborn and strong-willed people who passed their traits on to me. Thankfully, my husband saw only a glimpse of my *special* characteristics before he said, "I do." Depending on the situation, I can use these attributes for good; but in many instances, I can use them to get my own way. Serving in God's army, there is no room for one who wants to overrule the leader and take charge. Therefore, I need to subdue my strong-willed tendencies and submit to my commander—Jesus. This surrender does not come naturally to me or to you. Humans are selfish by nature and want their own way. Consequently, to relinquish my strong will and exchange it for God's perfect methods, daily I have to make a conscious choice to choose God over me. So must you.

Don't second guess Your commander.

Now that we've gotten ourselves out of the way, one important aspect of following any leader is the trust factor. Do you trust that God will protect you, shield you, and lead you in the right direction? Will He keep His promises to you? You can't follow a battle commander if you constantly second guess his decisions. If you have faith that God is sovereign and is in ultimate control over all happenings around you, then you are more apt to obey Him.

How do you get this kind of faith? In Romans 10:17 we read, *"So then faith comes by hearing, and hearing by the Word of God."* As with any successful battle strategy, you need accurate positioning. This scripture tells me that we all need to read God's Word and hear the Word preached and taught. We are not called to go it alone. We need each other. All of us should take the time to find a church that teaches God's Word with no apologies. At the church of your choosing, Jesus should be exalted as God's only Son, who died for our sins and rose again to rule in Heaven with His Father. Jesus is not *one* way, but the *only* way to heaven. If a church teaches any other doctrine than Jesus crucified, run away!

17

Position yourself To hear God.

With the proper positioning to hear God's Word about Jesus, you are one step closer to following voluntarily your leader in obedience. But what if your commander-in-chief tells you do to something that makes no sense? What then? Girlfriend, one thing you have to come to grips with is believing the Word of God from Genesis to the maps. There were approximately forty authors of the Bible who wrote the entire book over a period of about 1,500 years. Though men wrote down God's Words in the Bible, each word that God wanted in the Bible is in there; and all the words God wanted left out, are left out. God is sovereign, in control of everything in our world. Therefore, all the words found in the Bible can be trusted because they came from God. The scriptures are His very breath. There are no discrepancies or contradictions in the Bible. The people who spout this nonsense don't know the original Greek and Hebrew words of the Bible, or they would discover it all makes sense and is in no way conflicting.

The Bible should be your standard for testing everything else that claims to be true. You read the Bible not only to gain knowledge, but to apply His Word to your life so you can be equipped to do good works. In 2 Timothy 3:16 we read, "*All Scripture is given by inspiration of God, and is profitable for*

doctrine, for reproof, for correction, for instruction in
righteousness, that the man of God may be complete, thoroughly
equipped for every good work. " Let's take a moment to look more
closely at this verse.

- **Inspired by God**—breathed by God. He moved the writers
  to write His Words.
- **Doctrine**—It teaches us divine truth needed in life.
- **Reproof**—Scripture will expose our wrong behavior or
  wrong belief so that we can confess and repent.
- **Correction**—Not only will Scripture expose our sins, but it
  will point us back to godly living—a course correction.
- **Instruction**—The Scripture provides positive training in
  godly behavior. No person, book, organization, or
  government can supersede the authority of Scripture.

Now back to the dilemma of following orders that make no
sense. Guess what? God is God and I am not; therefore, He doesn't
have to give me all the details. But I am supposed to follow them.
I'm not sure where mankind got the idea that they had to know and
understand all the events that occur in their lives. God owes us no
explanations. Imagine that Noah had said he wasn't building an ark
because it was a dumb idea . . . there would be no humanity left.
Or if Moses had refused to follow God in the wilderness . . . the
Israelites would have either drowned in the Red Sea or been
slaughtered by Pharaoh's Egyptian army. If Ruth had failed to
follow God's leadership to go with Naomi, she wouldn't have met

19

and married Boaz—severing Jesus' lineage from the house of Jesse.

If you research Noah or Moses, you will read how disobedience by the people resulted in disaster every stinkin' time. Read a few books in the Old Testament, and you will understand what happens when one doesn't follow God's commands. There were times when the Israelites refused to listen to Noah and Moses, respectively. When the people didn't listen to their spiritual leaders, who were listening to God, they were easily deceived by the wrong voices. The Israelites followed their own desires even when it meant hurting others. They practiced witchcraft, soothsaying, idol worship, worship of the sun, moon, and stars, and sometimes they sacrificed their own children with fire.

Beware of Slippery slopes.

Permit me a sidebar here. If you read, study, or believe in horoscopes, you are on a slippery slope with Satan pulling you to the bottom. The definition of horoscope is "a forecast of a person's future, typically including a delineation of character and circumstances, based on the relative positions of the stars and planets at the time of that person's birth." You can read how King Saul, in 1 Chronicles 10, conferred with mediums for guidance instead of God. Saul died for his unfaithfulness. Always consult God when you need guidance—in all matters. Any activity, thought, or deed that goes against God's Word has Satan's fingerprints all over it, and it's meant to destroy you. Don't be deceived by what you think is a harmless activity—it is not! Thank you for that liberty; now let's continue in our study.

Sacrificing their children with fire, my word. How can people get so far from God you might wonder? The sad fact is that the Israelites kept repeating the same mistakes over and over and over again. We can learn from their failures by studying Biblical history so that we don't repeat their chief offense—disobedience to God. All of their tribulations pointed to this one offense. If they had obeyed God in all of His instructions, even when those directives didn't make sense to them, they could have avoided the horrible repercussions: broken lives, destroyed marriages, bitter disputes, slavery to sin, shame, guilt, a broken relationship with God, and even death. Do you find yourself staggering under the weight of consequences such as these?

As I write this chapter, there is a woman in Kentucky who made headline news when she refused to follow man's law that was polar opposite to God's law. Citing her Christian beliefs, she denied a marriage license to a same-sex couple. Courts deemed she was in willful violation of individuals' civil liberties. Her obedience to God brought great hardship to her and her family. She served time in jail, and certain groups of people tried to discredit her by sneering at her belief system. Her husband stood by her side in total support, but what did she stand to lose by taking a stand for Christ? Friends, family, her job, her reputation? We may never know the full extent of her losses. God never said obedience would be easy. This woman stood firm in her convictions prepared to receive criticism, discouragement, opposition, and maybe physical harm. One thing for certain: if she acted with a pure heart, God will use her story to glorify Him.

> # Root of disobedience
> # Is unbelief.

Charles Stanley said, "The real root of disobedience is unbelief. We disobey God when we do not believe either what He promises or what He instructs." Do not be caught being a stiff-necked woman. God created you, and He knows what is best for you. Obey Him, and He will bless you for it. I studied in 2 Kings, Chapter 18 about King Hezekiah who followed the Lord wholeheartedly with his obedience. You might think that it would be easy to follow God if you grew up in a king's palace. I need to mention that Hezekiah's father, Ahaz, had been one of the worst kings ever to rule Judah. If we based our conclusions on his childhood, Hezekiah would have been a terrible king. Instead, Hezekiah overcame his background and became a great leader because he relied on the Lord in every situation. He faithfully followed God during times of crisis and obeyed God's commands. As a result, God blessed Hezekiah and granted him success. At one point, God sent an avenging Angel who killed 185,000 fighting men of Assyria that threatened Hezekiah's kingdom. Now that was a great rescue!

Also in 2 Kings, Chapter 20, we read that King Hezekiah was sick unto death. Yet, again, Hezekiah cried out in prayer for God to remember his faithful obedience. God heard Hezekiah and added another fifteen years to his life. Hezekiah also asked God for a sign that he would live another fifteen years. God provided a sign by turning back the sun by ten steps. Wow! Can you imagine such a thing? You, too, can make a difference even if you are in the minority. Sincere faith and prayer to the one true God, can change any situation. Avoid the pitfalls of disobedience by choosing to obey God and watch how God blesses your life. Just remember your obedience must come from a willing and joyful heart—no playacting allowed.

Some of you reading this book might be new to faith in Jesus Christ. If you are unfamiliar with commands mentioned in the Bible, a good place to start is God's Ten Commandments found in Exodus 20:1-17. Most people have heard of the Ten Commandments even if they aren't knowledgeable about the Bible in general.

Exodus 20 vs. 3-6 "You shall have no other gods before me. . ."
This is what we discussed in Chapter one. God must have first
priority in our hearts. We can't have false gods or idols trying to
take God's place. For example, if I use my tithe to buy myself a
boat, then my boat has become my idol. I sin when I choose my
wants over giving a portion of my money to be used for God. If I
work sixty to seventy hours a week so I can buy more *stuff,* then
possessions have become my idol. If I'm obsessed with
electronics, money, sex, cars, or even Sunday sports and put them
ahead of God—they have become a false god. God created all
things, so bowing down to anything other than God is a sin. Take
stock of your life. Do you have any other gods in your life? Throw
them out, girlfriend.

OMG is
Not acceptable.

*Exodus 20 vs. 7 "You shall not take the name of the Lord your
God in vain, for the Lord will not hold him guiltless who takes His
name in vain."* Misusing God's name in any way is disparaging to
His character, His purposes, and His actions, which is the same as
lying about God. I pray you are not one who uses God's name in a
derogatory manner. Some think saying OMG is an acceptable
practice. In no way does saying or texting the words, *Oh My God,*

or the three letters, *OMG*, bring honor or glory to God. Unfortunately, those buzzwords are accepted in our society; and oftentimes, Christians are guilty of using them without thought. Don't allow those words to drip from your ruby-red lips or from your fingertips. It is not appropriate to God. If the way you use God's name is anything but honorable, stop it right now! It displeases God and breaks your communication with Him. In today's world you can't get away with cursing your commanding officer, so why would you think it is okay to use God's name in that way? Break that nasty habit!

Exodus 20 vs. 13 "You shall not murder." Gasp! You might be thinking, *I would never murder anyone!* I'm glad to hear it, but this goes beyond actually taking a life. In Matthew 15:19-20 we read, *"For out of the heart come evil thoughts, murders . . . these are the things which defile the man . . ."* A murderous thought toward another person is straight up murder in God's eyes. There are times when I'm angry at another person, and I say I want to stab them with an ice pick. Now, in actuality, I'm not really going to follow through with such a horrid act. However, God says don't even think it. Like you, I too must capture my evil thoughts and hold them captive, therefore, rescuing myself from murder.

Back in Chapter one, we covered the first and most important command in Matthew 22:37-38. Go ahead and re-read those verses in the first paragraph of Chapter one. Now read Matthew 22:39-40, *"And the second is like it: You shall love your neighbor as*

25

yourself. On these two commandments hang all the Law and the Prophets." This is a quotation from Leviticus 19:18 and the same idea as the Golden Rule found in Matthew 7:12. *"Therefore, whatever you want men to do to you, do also to them, for this is the Law and the Prophets.*" This particular command by Jesus summarized the ethical principles contained in the Law and the Prophets. You might not have realized it, but many of you learned this command in your childhood. Only it sounded more like this: Do unto others as you would have them do unto you. Or treat others the way you want to be treated. Either way, you were obeying a command of Jesus. That's always a good thing.

These are only a few of the important instructions of God. I don't want you bogged down into thinking the Christian life is all about following rules and commands. However, when you have a true collision with Christ, you are a changed person. The commands in the Bible are not viewed as burdensome. Instead, pleasing Him becomes an important life goal which results in obedience to Him.

Take a breath and let this chapter sink into your psyche. You might want to re-read some of the verses listed here to get the full impact about obedience. When you choose to obey your commanding officer, He will take full responsibility for any consequences that result from your obedience. So march on following the ultimate leader, Jesus Christ.

Paul wrote in Romans 7:19, *"For the good that I will to do, I do not do; but the evil I will not to do, that I practice."* Today, if you strive to be obedient, sign and date this page.

Date_____Signature_____

DIG DEEPER

Chapter 2

1. Which part of your Godly armor needs repair work? Why?

2. What is one problem you need to give to God's control?

3. What church do you attend? What made you choose it?

4. Remember a time when you disobeyed God's Word. What were the consequences?

5. Sight a time when you obeyed God and the blessings that came from your obedience.

6. What or who tries to be first in your life ahead of God?

Chapter 3

Enemy Attack!

Congratulations! You've made it into the trenches of obedience. Sit tight. You are deep in enemy territory. Hunkered down in obedience can provide a hedge of protection that you're going to need. When you choose to put God first and to obey His commands, it makes Satan fighting mad. Satan will have to work harder to make you feel discouraged, hopeless, frustrated, angry, or disgusted with life; but he's up for the challenge. Stick close to God. He will prepare you for any attack.

God knows when you choose to obey Him that life is not going to turn out ideally. In fact, many times, hardships seem to be the outcome. Why? Why do bad things seem to happen to those who are trying to do good? Why does the world hate those of us who follow Jesus and do good to our fellow man? That doesn't seem fair.

Keith and I were married four years when we began preparation for our first child. Before he was born, we poured over baby books trying to choose the best name. Finally, after months of deliberation, we settled on Aaron. The perfect name for the perfect child. Right? Once Aaron was born, we found out he had a heart defect. Why had God allowed that to happen to our precious baby boy? Keith was a full-time minister who studied the scriptures, preached, cared for people, witnessed to the lost, and comforted the grieving. I taught pre-school Sunday school, sang in the choir, sang in an ensemble, served as Baptist young women's president, counseled hurting women, among other activities. We both were trying to put God first and follow His commands. So what went wrong? You might be asking yourself the same type of questions about your situation. Why God? Why me and why now?

First, you need to know that God never, and I mean never, makes mistakes. Nothing catches Him off guard. He is Omnipresent—present everywhere at once. He is Omnipotent—all powerful. He is Omniscient—knowing all things. Anything that touches your life has gone through God's fingers first. With that in mind, we come back to the haunting question. Why?

Our next stop was a visit to the cardiologist, Dr. Bargeron. He showed us ultra sound images of our son's heart as he explained the procedure needed to fix the problems. We vividly remember his asking us if we understood what he was saying. He seemed perplexed when we remained calm. It was a wonderful opportunity to tell Dr. Bargeron how only through our God's sustaining power were we able to remain peaceful in the midst of this horrendous storm. Aaron didn't have just one hole in his heart; he had two plus a malfunctioning valve. Our precious baby would need open heart surgery to repair his heart.

Naturally, Keith and I prayed for God to heal our son's heart without surgery. We enlisted thousands of people to pray for a miracle in Aaron's life, but God said "no" to a miraculous healing. Instead, God used doctors, nurses, and other hospital staff to repair Aaron's heart defects. He is now a healthy husband and a father of his own rambunctious son and baby girl. Since we've already established that God has a plan, one question remains. What was God's reason for it?

> There's purpose
> in the pain.

I often quote Dr. Tony Evans, a Christian pastor, speaker, author and widely syndicated radio and television broadcaster in the United States. Dr. Tony Evans says, "When it's not fair, it doesn't mean God's not there. Trust Him. He has a purpose in the pain." As Keith and I searched for answers, we found some reasons as to why bad things happen and how followers of Christ are to deal with them.

First, we need to go all the way back to Genesis when Adam and Eve ate the fruit from the Tree of Knowledge. God had specifically told them not to eat of that tree or they would die. Up until the very first bite of the forbidden fruit, Adam and Eve were perfect people, living in a perfect paradise, enjoying a perfect relationship with God. Life was blissful.

Then entered the cunning serpent who said to Eve in Genesis 3:4-5, "*You will not surely die. For God knows that in the day you eat of it your eyes will be opened, and you will be like God, knowing good and evil.*" If you read Chapters one and two of Genesis, you know that everything God created was good, even a serpent. However, Satan manipulated and used the serpent to question God's command and then appealed to Eve's vanity—she could be like God. Once Adam and Eve ate the outlawed fruit, sin entered the world and with it came destruction in the form of sickness, disease, pain, anger, jealousy, envy, conflict, hate, and all other factors of evil. Unfortunately, these consequences will last until Jesus returns.

As you just read, God didn't cause sickness and disease to enter into the world; it was all Satan. Immediately, after the first little nibble, Adam and Eve found out that disobeying God resulted in tragedy, not in blessings. Instantly, they severed their intimate relationship with God. There was now a barrier between them and

God . . . SIN. Knowing this Bible history, Keith and I didn't shake our fists at God and demand to know why He had caused our son's heart condition because He hadn't. However, we did wonder why God allowed it.

Look Inward

One place to look when disaster strikes is inward. Is there unconfessed sin in your life that has caused your horrible state of affairs? With Adam and Eve, there is no doubt that their sin caused damaging consequences. What about you and your circumstances? Are you struggling with hardship? You might need a heart check. For instance, you could be harboring unforgiveness close to your heart. This smoldering sin can quickly turn into bitterness that can sneak out at home or at work through an ugly spirit. Are you too bossy, too judgmental, too jealous, too angry, too prideful, too hardhearted, too greedy . . . you get the picture. When sin goes unchecked, it eventually affects all of your relationships in one way or another. Any sin that you hold onto will produce nasty results. You, too, might need heart surgery. Take an inventory of your heart and cut away those things that displease God. You know what they are. Confess and carve them out!

Trial by Fire

Not always is sin the culprit for our suffering. To paraphrase
Tony Evans, God has a purpose for our pain. If you ever wonder
how strong your faith is in God, you'll find out when you pass
through a fire, not a literal fire, but a trial by fire. Keith and I have
had our share of *trial by fire* sessions. We have survived sickness,
cancer, multiple surgeries, financial problems, death of parents,
trauma from numerous moves, changing schools, and assorted
heartaches. There were many other trials, but I have chosen to
forget them. Thankfully, God had a time limit on each one.

Are you in the midst of a fiery trial? You might have lost a
loved one which left a hole in your heart so big you fear you might
never recover. Or perhaps you find yourself in a financial crisis.
You wonder how you can pay your bills and feed your children at
the same time. Maybe you're experiencing a debilitating disease
where the cure seems worse than the disease. Or worse, you have a
wayward child who places himself in danger by using drugs or
alcohol, and you wonder how it ever came to this end.

We live in a fallen, sinful world. Expect heartaches to come
your way, but remember you don't have to go it alone. God wants
to use that time to draw you closer to Him because He has the
solution. He possesses the power to work in your situation. Seek
Him. God also created professionals to come along beside you
through your storm. He has provided numerous organizations to
aid and support you in your time of need. Don't allow pride to hold

you back from getting the assistance you require. One important truth to hold tight is that your calamity is on God's timetable, and the clock is ticking down.

A Focus Adjustment

Looking back on our hardships, I can see how we grew spiritually through each instance. God was molding Keith and me to be more like Jesus. He also proved how insufficient we were without Him. There are times when each of us feels confident in our own abilities, and we plow through life without consulting God about our activities. Then, *wha-la*, you become mired down with a messy life and quickly find out you can't do life on your own. You need God's help, strength, wisdom, and deliverance. You see, there are times when God needs to get your attention; and He will do whatever it takes to get you fixated on Him. Therefore, He allows some adversities into your life to wake you up, to redirect your focus away from yourself and back toward Jesus.

Whenever our family of four was going through a rough patch, we often called a family meeting. By the way, our kids loathed these meetings. During our meeting we often asked this question: whose attention is God trying to get? Then we looked at one another to see who would confess. It makes me smile now; but at the time when we were fighting the blazing trial, it was serious. Keith would comment that we were experiencing character building days. Our son was quick to point out he had enough character. Remember, you learned in the first chapter that God wants to be first in your life. Don't push God out of your life, or He just might send an intense test to get your attention.

Future Preparation

There are times when God allows or causes a struggle to invade your pleasant, rockin'-a-long life to prepare you for something in the future. At the time of Aaron's surgery, he was only twenty-one months old. We had prayed all those months that God would heal Aaron without surgery, but God had other plans. The night before his surgery, I spent the night in Aaron's hospital room while Keith and our parents were in a near-by hotel. Aaron slept after receiving a sedative for the night. The room was quite dark, and I couldn't see to read. I went into the bathroom and sat on the edge of the tub. I cried and prayed for our son, not understanding God's reason, but trusting Him anyway. While there I read Psalm 23 and 24 and clung to God's promises. He would be the mighty warrior who would protect and care for our baby during surgery. God reminded me that Aaron had been entrusted to Keith and me for a season, and God would be the One to determine how long that season would last.

As I emerged into the darkened room, I had a runny nose and red, scratchy eyes; but I was at peace. This twenty-six year-old mother had been on emotional waves for twenty-one months—praying for a miracle. A light from the hallway illuminated

Aaron's bed allowing me to gaze upon his smooth chest. I dreaded what he would endure but was relieved to know God was in control. Whatever the outcome, God would use it for His glory; and Keith and I would survive the ordeal. God had promised it in His Word.

If you've never been in this type of scenario, you might not realize that parents become friends with other parents in the same situation. The next morning Aaron went into surgery while we waited in a special room with our parents. There was a tangible peace that permeated the room all because hundreds of people were praying for us. Right after Aaron's surgery, another little boy had surgery. Aaron survived, but that young boy did not. God positioned Keith and me to minister to this family from out-of-state. He gave us ample opportunities to counsel and pray with this devastated father and mother. Thankfully, they too were Christians and possessed God's peace and comfort. Life can be an uphill battle. Even though God never vowed an easy life, He did promise to help us, comfort us, anchor us, fight for us, protect us, empower us, uphold us, and be the lifter of our heads. As I said previously, none of us were created to go it alone. We need God, and we need each other.

Surviving each ordeal builds our faith as we experience God's sustaining power in our lives. I'm so thankful God limits how long we suffer with each trial. He works out His plan and teaches us along each arduous step. Psalm 34:10 says, *"Many are the afflictions of the righteous. But the Lord delivers him out of them all."* As we humorously say in our family, hurry up and learn what God wants to teach you so we can get out of this mess and move on.

Before we continue, let's recap what we have discussed in this chapter. When you feel like you are under attack by the enemy, look to your commander and discern His tactics.

Possible reasons for an attack, trial, suffering, sorrow, or pain:

1. Do you have personal sin you need to confess?
2. Is God testing your faith?
3. Are you needing to grow spiritually?
4. Have you lost your focus? Do you need to give God first place in your life?
5. Is your strength insufficient? Do you need Godly strength and help?
6. Is God stretching and molding you to be more like Jesus?
7. Will your experience be used to help others?
8. Do you need to rest in the Father's arms and receive peace?
9. Will God be glorified when you complete the trial?
10. How will God use it for your good?

Romans 5:3-4 says *". . . but we also glory in tribulations, knowing that tribulation produces perseverance; and perseverance, character; and character, hope."*

Today, if you choose to take your trials to God and seek His help, sign and date this page.

Date_____Signature_____

DIG DEEPER

Chapter 3

1. In what way do you feel attacked? What defensive action can you take?

2. What has seemed like a logical action to take only to have it bite you in the end?

3. Are you holding on to a sin? If so, what is it?

4. What fiery trial has tested your faith?

5. In what way is God trying to get your attention?

6. Who comes alongside of you to help you through your storms?

Chapter 4

Who's Got Your Back?

There's no doubt about it—we are under attack by the enemy. Our opponent lies, deceives, steals, kills, and prepares sneak attacks. In 1 Peter 5:8 we read, *"Be sober, be vigilant; because your adversary the devil walks about like a roaring lion, seeking whom he may devour."* Hopefully, you have agreed that in order to develop a counterattack against your adversary, you have to listen and obey your leader. There's another critical decision you must make in order to survive—who's got your back?

During war, soldiers are highly trained for combat. They go through extensive drills to make sure each person can execute his job without hesitation. Every little detail is important for survival. Whether you are a private or a colonel, everyone works together to battle the enemy. Many times they take the position of bounding overwatch or leapfrogging. This maneuver is where one soldier moves forward while another soldier shoots to protect the one on the move. Needless to say, the entire unit functions as an organism working together to stay alive. Each person puts his trust in another to watch his back. In today's world, that's the type of person I want by my side.

Thankfully, most people reading this book will never go into a battle using a machine gun or an assault rifle. However, we each encounter real battles every day. For some of us the giants we fight might be cancer, divorce, betrayal, gossip, financial ruin, disappointment, hopelessness, or any number of problems that crash into our organized world. Therefore, it's beneficial to have a trusted friend to call upon in times of trouble. Your first line of defense should always be to cry out to God. Once you have poured out your heart to Him and sought His wisdom, it's good to find a friend with skin who can be a great comfort. Many times that person will be your husband for those who are married; on other occasions you just need to have a heart-to-heart chat with a trustworthy girlfriend. Ahh . . . a trustworthy friend . . . now finding one of those can be a challenge.

Let me insert an important condition about friends. If you are a woman, aside from your husband, your best friends should be women. Never find yourself confiding personal information to another man especially if he, too, is married. This practice will set you both up to fall into sin. I know some readers are rolling their eyes at my advice. Let me assure you, after forty years in Christian ministry with my husband, this type of relationship ends in disaster. We've watched mature Christians and even pastors ruin their lives from choosing to confide in persons of the opposite sex. Think of when your parents told you to stay back from a fire to avoid getting burned—same principle here. Now that I've cautioned you, I expect you to heed my words of warning.

Be Careful and Selective!

When choosing our girlfriends, we need to be careful and selective. Not everyone who is fun to be around is suitable as a close friend. I'm not talking about acquaintances, but *". . . a friend who sticks closer than a brother"* as found in Proverbs 18:24. You might be wondering what the criteria should be for choosing an honorable comrade. As always, the Bible provides many examples about friendship.

Do you remember the story about Job? If not, let me just say that he had a bucket full of life issues to deal with; and he had *friends* who were more than happy to offer their advice. His three closest friends, who he thought were going to come to his aid when disaster struck, weren't what they seemed. Let me give you a brief rundown on his life and his so-called "friends."

Job was a wealthy man who feared God and shunned evil. He had seven sons and three daughters along with much wealth: 7,000 sheep, 3,000 camels, 500 oxen, 500 female donkeys, and a large household. He was considered the greatest man of all the people in the East at this point in history. Satan petitioned God to allow him to attack Job. Satan claimed that God had a hedge of protection around Job but, if Job lost all he had, Job would curse God. So the battle began.

God allowed Satan to persecute and accuse Job, but there was a limit to the amount of adversity Satan was allowed to inflict on Job. Satan was forbidden to kill Job. With rapid-fire disasters, Satan destroyed his children, his livestock, his servants, and compromised Job's health, leaving him with a painful, riddled-of-disease body. Needless to say, Job was devastated. His wife was the only family member who survived. Now your problems might not compare to Job's—his were over the top—but, I daresay, you know the feel of excruciating heartache.

After Job's disasters struck, his three friends appeared on the scene: Eliphaz, Bildad, and Zophar. At first his friends came beside him to mourn and offer comfort for his anguish—definitely pleasing characteristics of a friend. His agony was so great that the three men were speechless for seven days and nights. Do you have friends like these? Ones who will offer their support without saying a word? Such friends are priceless.

Job was in constant agony both physically and emotionally. His groans and cries poured out like water, yet he knew that God had His sovereign hand on his life. Eliphaz was the first to speak. He spoke profoundly and gently but had no clue what was happening in the Heavenly realm. He accused Job of being guilty of some serious sin that was causing him to reap God's anger. He encouraged Job to confess and repent so that God would bless him with prosperity, security, family, and a rich life. Eliphaz went on to indicate that Job was not holy enough and that he didn't have proper reverence for God. He expounded on how great and wise God is, yet his accusations against Job were wrong. Beware— sometimes friends can appear to be wise on occasion when, in fact, they are behaving foolishly. Even the devil mixes truth with lies to make his point. We must discern what is truth and what is not. Don't be swayed by eloquent words spoken by a friend. You have to discern if her words are supported by Godly principles. Does her everyday walk exhibit that she is following God's instructions for her own life? If not, how are these "friends" qualified to give you advice?

Remember that every time something bad happens to you doesn't mean that it's a result of a sin. Not every painful episode we reap is a consequence of something we've sown. Well-meaning friends can give you bad direction when trying to explain why bad things are happening in your life. Again ask yourself if they are following after God's own heart in the matter or just spouting off worldly advice that doesn't line up with God's Word.

Swift to hear! Slow to speak!

In James 1:19 we read, *"So then, my beloved brethren, let every man be swift to hear, slow to speak, slow to wrath; for the wrath of man does not produce the righteousness of God."*
We want those closest to us to be kind and compassionate. Those who are quick to hear about our sorrows, yet slow to offer advice to alleviate the situation are desired as our companions. There are appropriate times to give guidance to someone in trouble; then, there are times just to listen and provide support. A wise friend knows the difference.

The next guy, Bildad, was not a friend I would want in my camp. He judged Job without having all the facts. He implied that Job's sons must have deserved what happened to them and that Job needed to quit complaining. What a horrible thing to say! He went on to say that Job's anger at God was causing Job's trouble. Job was extremely distraught, yet Bildad buried him with more disturbing accusations. Have you ever had a friend who judged you? Or maybe you have judged others with unmerited charges. Judging is up to God. You may have an opinion, but not all opinions should be shared. Watch out for people who set themselves up as "know-it-alls" capable of judging your actions or deeds.

Lastly, Zophar decided to weigh in on Job's problems. He agreed with Bildad and Eliphaz that Job was guilty of sin and remained unrepentant. He insulted Job and essentially called him a fool and a sinner who wouldn't admit the obvious truth. Zophar's implications were that Job was wicked, hypocritical, and proud and that he had caused his own dire consequences. Have you ever had a friend who got angry with you because you wouldn't see what they saw as the reason for your difficulty? It's not profitable to have a friend who assesses your circumstances without knowing the whole situation or all the facts. As we read, Job's friends had knowledge and even godly knowledge, but such information doesn't always equate to true wisdom.

When I was thirty-three years old, I knew a Christian woman, whom I'll call Diana, who claimed to be my friend; but her actions and words did not prove her to be who she claimed to be. She was well versed in the Bible, but she lacked wisdom on how to apply that knowledge. Diana had befriended me when Keith accepted a ministerial position at her church. As the newest staff wife, I was elated to have a friend. For over two years we walked together, our kids played together, and our families shared meals. However, as a result of Diana's and her husband's disagreeing with the pastor, they joined others in attacking the pastor's character. Witnessing

47

the negative turn in her attitude, I decided to sever what had become an unhealthy relationship. Let me just say—it's unwise to mess with God's anointed. I wanted no part of it!

One day my path crossed with Diana's in the grocery store. I stood speechless when she verbally attacked me as I placed green beans in my basket. Let's just say she judged my motives and actions as mean-spirited when I had ceased to call her. But she didn't stop there. The venom spewing from her lips was shocking. No one had ever said such hateful words to me and in such a public setting. Tears sprang to my eyes as I remained paralyzed on isle three. Mortified, I watched as other shoppers passed by with looks of horror upon their faces—Diana was not quiet! Once she finished slicing me with her sharp tongue, she stormed off leaving me stunned. After a moment, I staggered away on shaking legs, anxious to leave the store.

Those hateful remarks flowed from Diana's hurt feelings and her heart of anger. Matthew 15:18 says, *"But those things which proceed out of the mouth come from the heart, and they defile a man."* With God's direction, I concentrated on holding back a snapping retort and vowed to use greater care in choosing future friends. Our grocery-store encounter reinforced the wisdom of distancing myself from a toxic person no matter the consequences.

Eliphaz, Bildad, and Zophar's theological words missed the mark. All three of them agreed that God was powerful, wise, and sovereign; but their traits for friendship fell short of what it means to be a worthy friend. These guys offered unwise advice, were quick to judge, mixed truth with lies, and used eloquent words that lacked truth. These men are not the type of pals you want protecting your back. However, the Bible has great examples of companions with commendable attributes.

Commendable Attributes!

One of the greatest stories in the Bible on friendship is the one found in 1 Samuel of David and Jonathan found. Jonathan was the son of King Saul and David was a subject of King Saul. After David slew Goliath, Saul set him over the men of war. Jonathan and David were polar opposites in terms of social standing and education. Jonathan had been privy to all that the royal family possessed while David had grown up as a shepherd boy under the guidance of a Godly father. What an unlikely pair to become beloved companions!

In Chapter 18 of 1 Samuel, we find that Jonathan loved David as a brother with loyalty and devotion. They both worshipped the same God; and even though Jonathan was the prince of Israel and heir to the throne, he discerned that David was special and made a covenant with him. We see how the love of a friend can grow and blossom with ease when both are walking the same path in the same direction. When the Lord is the centerpiece of your relationship, you will have the best of friendships.

Let's go back to my serious matter. Before you start feeling sorry for me because I lost a good friend, I had other friends who were true to their faith walk. One sweet woman, whom I'll call Sally, was particularly helpful to me. When I called to unload my burden, she silently listened without interruption or passing any type of judgment and allowed me to cry out from the depth of my anguish. After I had emptied my heart, she calmly replied with Godly wisdom. Sally directed me back to God's Word and what I knew to be true: God still loved me, God would work out good for me even though it might be a painful process, and no matter how many judgmental people crossed my path, God was my ultimate judge. Actually, He is the only One qualified to do the job. Sally assured me she would diligently pray for me and my family. My imperfections and insecurities were filtered through her "spiritual" goggles, helping me to view my situation the way God saw it. She had my back. Sally was the epitome of a Godly friend who loved me like a sister and treated me with kindness and compassion. Today we are still close friends even though separated by hundreds of miles.

The deep love Jonathan felt for David caused him to put his life at risk to protect David. Several times Jonathan spoke up in defense of David when King Saul wanted to kill David out of jealousy. Jonathan spoke well of David even though King Saul was angry that they were friends. More than once, Jonathan risked his own life to defend David and help him escape death. Jonathan went on to strengthen and encourage David's faith by providing his help and continued support in the midst of a possible murder attempt by his own father, King Saul. Do you have a friend who would risk possible danger in order to keep you safe? One who encourages you and imparts Godly wisdom to you during trials? One who is loyal and speaks truth into your life? That is a rare kind of friend and one to be cherished.

In the end, David grieved intensely over Jonathan's death when he was killed by the enemy. The two of them had shared a strong bond that was noble, loyal, and selfless. David wrote a song about King Saul and his son, Jonathan, to be taught through the ages. The song honored King Saul, but it *celebrated* his dear friend, Jonathan.

True Friendship!

Even when I wrote this chapter, a story captured my attention as an act of friendship, similar to David and Jonathan, was played out on the international stage. Twelve boys and their coach, "Ake," were trapped in a popular destination called Tham Luang Cave in Thailand. The soccer team went exploring to celebrate one member's birthday. The coach saw their bikes and went in to find them. Unfortunately, they were surprised by the July monsoon season beginning on June 23, 2018. Their plight gained national attention as volunteers from across the globe flew to Thailand to assist. Cave divers arrived June on 28 unsure if the boys were even alive. On July 2 divers found all thirteen alive two and a half miles from the cave entrance.

Forced farther into the cave by the rushing waters, the boys and coach had used rocks to carve a deeper shelf on which to huddle together and keep warm. Their twenty-five-year-old coach had taught them meditation to help calm them and use less oxygen. They had limited drinkable water yet survived in darkness for nine days. When found, the boys were in no way frantic or scared—just cold and hungry!

For nine days Ake had managed to keep his team peaceful in the face of looming danger and uncertainty as water lapped near their feet. During those days, the coach gave up his ration of water to the boys. When discovered, Ake was the weakest but insisted he be the last one extracted during the incredible recovery. His concern and love for those twelve boys was evident as he put them before his own life. Much like David and Jonathan, their story was one of hope, survival, and true friendship in the face of peril. Please take the time to read the total story about this miraculous rescue. You'll see God's hand at work.

Can you have a close friend that is not a Christian? Absolutely. If you only associate with other Christians, there is a flaw in your plan. God calls us to be the salt and light to a lost world. Just keep in mind that the counsel non-Christians offer you will not be based on Godly wisdom, but on worldly views and their own opinion. It doesn't make what they say necessarily wrong or bad advice, just not Godly. You'll need to filter their words through God's principles. You should have a variety in the ages of your friends, as well. When Keith and I went to serve at his first church, some of our first and closest friends to this day were older than the two of us. They served as mentors to two young people who needed help and advice in all aspects of life. It's also good to have companions who are similar to your stage of life such as: children, jobs, likes and dislikes, values, morals. However, if you have five or fewer close friends, you are blessed. Those are the guys you can call in the middle of the night during an emergency or the ones who will keep your children with them all night when you are in the hospital.

Relationships built on love and trustworthiness are a rare treasure. True friends are faithful in times of adversity as well as success. Proverbs 17:17 says: *"A friend loves at all times, and a brother is born for adversity."* Being a friend and having a friend involves some risk. You don't know a person deeply until you've experienced much together. Even a Christian friend can allow pride and selfishness to invade the friendship and cause great harm. Other times God uses wise counselors to help us find His will for our lives. We just need to double check and make sure their counsel lines up with the Word of God. Remember that those closest to us greatly influence our lives—especially our spiritual lives. Since friends help shape our spiritual destinies, we must choose wisely!

<u>So what characteristics are important for the friends "guarding your back?"</u>

1. One who can offer support and comfort you—sometimes without saying a word
2. One whose walk reflects her closeness to God
3. One who tells the truth in love
4. One who treats people with kindness no matter who that person is
5. One who possesses similar values and morals that you hold dear
6. One who withholds judgment until she knows all the facts and then offers Godly advice
7. One who is a good listener—quick to hear
8. One who doesn't allow selfish pride to cause harm to the relationship
9. One who brings joy to your life
10. One who is willing to give up her desires in order to put your needs first during a trial

John 15:13 *"Greater love has no one than this, than to lay down one's life for his friends."*

Today I desire first to be a friend of Jesus and then to be the type of friend that everyone wants to gain. May I be found faithful to the task.

Date _____ Signature_____

DIG DEEPER

Chapter 4

1. What has caused you excruciating heartache? Who helped you the most?

2. Who do you count as a wise friend? Is this person different from your BFF? If so, why?

3. Who is your best friend and why? List your close friends and the values you share.

4. Are you a good listener? If not, why not? Explain

5. Are you the type of friend others want to gain? Why or why not?

Chapter 5

Quick, Grab the Rubies!

By now you probably are aware that the enemy is relentless. He continues to hound you as you strive to follow God in righteousness and to put God first in your life. The closer you draw to God, the more Satan is infuriated. So what's a girl to do? It's time to tap into one of God's most powerful resources—wisdom—Godly wisdom!

Before we delve into how to gain Godly wisdom, let's define two words. Webster says wisdom is "the quality of being wise; the power of judging rightly and following the soundest course of action, based on knowledge, experience, understanding, etc." Note in this definition that wisdom and knowledge are two different things. Knowledge is "acquaintance with facts; range of information, awareness, or understanding." We live in the most educated culture in the history of the world, yet our culture is collapsing all around us. We're drowning in data, yet wisdom is waning. We have more knowledge at our fingertips than ever before, yet we're walking the path of foolishness. It's time to change this downward spiral. You've made a positive step by committing to apply the Godly principles to your life mentioned in this book. Let's add another layer of protection by studying the proverbs of the wisest human on earth—King Solomon.

I hate to start out with bad news, but no one is born with Godly wisdom. You might possess worldly wisdom, but you have to be a lover of God to be in the position to receive His wisdom. With that in mind, if we're not born with it, how do we get it? Proverbs 9:10 says, *"The fear of the Lord is the beginning of wisdom, and the knowledge of the Holy One is understanding."* Oftentimes, Christians are confused when the Bible says to fear God. Does it mean we have to tremble in fear of God in order to get Godly wisdom? Absolutely not! It's healthy for us to fear sinning because we know God hates sin or to fear the consequences of our sins because God judges our unrighteousness. However, the fear found in Proverbs 9:10 is a fear that shows reverence and awe for our Almighty God, the Creator of all things. Oswald Chambers says, "The remarkable thing about fearing God is that, when you fear God, you fear nothing else; whereas, if you do not fear God, you fear everything else."

SEEK WISDOM!

There are steps you can take to acquire Godly wisdom.
Proverbs 2:6 reads, *"For the Lord gives wisdom; From His mouth
come knowledge and understanding."* As you can see, wisdom's
starting points are God and His revealed Word. It's seeing our
world from God's point of view and responding to the world using
His written Word by applying His principles. The Bible tells us
that God's wisdom is hidden from the rebellious and the foolish—
those who don't love Him. It's reserved for those who love Him.
As one of His children, you have to put in the effort to find
wisdom and to use it. This is not a one-and-done type of search.

Have you ever been on a scavenger hunt? You know, where
you're given a map or clues and once you've meticulously
followed all the evidence without deviation, you find the treasure
which might be chocolates or ice cream? In Proverbs 8:11 we read,
*"For wisdom is better than rubies, and all the things one may
desire cannot be compared with her."* Just as you dig to uncover
precious jewels, you must dig through God's Word to become
wise. His Word is our map to treasures untold. You can't walk
wisely if you never open the Bible. There are no short cuts. Don't
abandon the search when you come to a difficult road. It's a daily
process of choosing between two paths—one is wicked and the

other is righteous. Each time you choose the path of righteousness you uncover another valuable jewel.

This wisdom is available for every believer. You don't have to attend church every Sunday or participate in every Bible study offered by your church to get it. There's no prerequisite of praying at the altar or singing in the choir. As far as I know, there's no celestial report card that requires all A's in order to receive Godly wisdom. In Proverbs 8:17, wisdom says, *"I love those who love me, and those who seek me diligently will find me."* God will give His wisdom to those who earnestly seek it. Start digging!

GAIN WITH GROWTH!

We gain wisdom through a constant process of growing. We grow spiritually by studying God's Word, meditating on His Word, obeying His principles, and applying those principles to our lives. From this practice, we not only try to stop doing evil, but we also hate the evil we once did. This wisdom God speaks about is for the heart. Since the womb of the heart is capable of growing evil or nurturing good, we must make right choices to avoid moral pitfalls. It's a lifelong series of right choices. What happens when you make stupid or bad decisions? Fear not. You are not doomed. Recognize your error, repent, and get back on the right path.

Remember when we talked about meditating on God's Word back in Chapter 1? We need to keep His Word close to our heart—treasure it—for true wisdom is applying knowledge in a life-changing way. Proverbs 2:1, 5 reads, *"My son, if you receive my Words, and treasure my commands within you . . . then you will understand the fear of the Lord, and find the knowledge of God."* When I treasure an item, I take extra-special care of it, I desire it, I protect it, and I guard it. Do you treasure God's Word?

If you struggle with finances, marital conflict, rebellious children, or which direction to take on your life's path, you need Godly wisdom. If you're physically or mentally ill—you need Godly wisdom. If you're not sure which job to accept—you need Godly wisdom. If you struggle to set life goals—you need Godly wisdom. Do you see a pattern here? Carve out time to study Jesus' ministry, or Paul's journeys, or Moses' leadership, or Solomon's wisdom, or the Israelites' journey. You will gain insights and advice on how to apply their principles to your life circumstances. Get into the mind of God by growing spiritually, and you'll be able to see what He thinks about your situation.

In this chapter concerning wisdom, I often refer to the Book of Proverbs. Twenty-nine chapters in Proverbs are a collection of teachings from Solomon to his son, showing the young man how to live a godly life in an ungodly world. Solomon had learned that trying to solve life's problems without God's help is foolish. These truisms are not divine promises or guarantees but warnings to live prudently. When we follow God's principles and guidelines outlined in the Bible, the usual result is blessings. Be a Solomon today!

WILLINGLY OBEY HIS WORD!

Hand in hand with gaining Godly wisdom through spiritual growth is a willingness to obey His Word. Remember, we discussed this in Chapter 2. If I'm not willing to obey God's Word, then I'm living in sin. I can't continue sinning and expect to gain wisdom from God. According to the Bible, it can't happen. He expects me to read and study His truths and then apply them to my life. This process allows me to test His truths to see if they work.

Proverbs 2:7 reads, *"He stores up sound wisdom for the upright; He is a shield to those who walk uprightly."* When I walk in His Will through obedience, then evil, immorality, perversity, and other temptations will no longer appeal to me. I might stumble, but I will learn from my mistakes because He stores up wisdom for the upright. The important concept is to practice obedience even during difficult times and watch how God provides.

In 1982, we were a two-income family. Keith was a minister and I worked as an accountant where my business world revolved around numbers balancing. When our son had open heart surgery, I temporarily stopped working to stay home and care for him. Let me just say, at twenty-six years old, I was a wee-bit spiritually immature . . . what am I saying? I was a whole lot spiritually immature. After several weeks of my son's recovery, the medical bills began to appear in our mailbox. As I sifted through those debts and looked at our bank balance, I couldn't see how we were to pay the growing sums without my income. Thankfully, I had a husband who trusted wholly in God's provisions. He never wavered in his commitment to continue tithing even though I looked on chewing my nails. For Keith trusting God came natural; but, for me, the situation was a test.

The world's wisdom told me to pay my hospital debts first; and if I had any money left afterwards, give an offering to God. Malachi 3:8 says, *"Will a man rob God? Yet you have robbed Me! But you say, 'In what way have we robbed you?' In tithes and offerings."* Malachi goes on to say in verse 10, *"Bring all the tithes into the storehouse, that there may be food in My house, and try Me now in this,"* says the Lord of hosts, *"If I will not open for you the windows of heaven and pour out for you such blessing, that there will not be room enough to receive it."* Oh dear!

This young wife and mother stepped out in faith and wrote the tithe check each week. Through obedience, I put God's principles to the test. Would He provide for our needs or would I serve up shoe leather for our dinner? As His Word says, obedience brings blessings. We paid all of our household bills; and within a year, we had fulfilled all hospital and doctor obligations. God provided in ways we never imagined. Several doctors accepted the insurance compensation as full payment relieving us of any obligation—a rare occurrence. We recognized it as God at work. Stepping out in faith and doing what God's Word prompted, we received gladly the blessings He poured out on us.

With any of us, when we respond to God's commands in our daily lives, we bear witness of His greatness. In this instance, we chose to set aside what the world commonly practices and instead honored God with our obedience. People in the world who don't fear God might look sideways at your decisions when you follow God's directions. Ignore them. His way is best!

ASK FOR IT!

Ask for it? Yes, pray for God to give you His wisdom. One of God's promises is found in James 1:5. *"If any of you lacks wisdom, let him ask of God, who gives to all liberally and without reproach, and it will be given to him."* You need to know that James, the half-brother of Jesus, was talking to Jewish believers living outside of Judea among the Gentiles. Seldom accepted by their countrymen, these Jews were often abused by the Gentiles. These believers knew a thing or two about difficult conditions. They needed wisdom to know what to do in the middle of such confusing circumstances—clarity only God could provide.

In this verse, liberally means "stretching out." Think of it as a banquet table loaded down with delicious pieces of wisdom that God made available for His children. It's a feast that never runs out. To eat from this bountiful offering you don't have to attend church every week, or visit five lost souls per week, or volunteer in the nursery during worship. No! God is generous with His wisdom for every believer; but He waits. He waits for you to ask.

When we ask God for His wisdom, we need to pray with a humble attitude. We can't come demanding that He give us wisdom especially if we're being disobedient children. He stores up wisdom for us, but receiving it is based upon the kind of life we're living. If I put my own desires above pleasing God, if I make decisions without consulting God, or if I knowingly sin on a consistent basis, I would be arrogant to ask God to dump His wisdom on me. I need to take stock of my life choices and start doing what God's already told me to do through His Word.

When you pray for God's divine wisdom, know that it goes beyond common sense. You can have common sense and still not understand how to choose joy in the middle of trials. Yet, wisdom allows you to do just that. As I pointed out in the first paragraphs, it begins with respect for God, but results in the ability to tell right from wrong.

James, Chapter 3:17 says, *"But the wisdom that is from above is first pure, then peaceable, gentle, willing to yield, full of mercy and good fruits, without partiality and without hypocrisy."*

Wisdom is pure—based upon God's holiness. He is incapable of producing evil.

Wisdom is peaceable—a blessing available from God alone.

Wisdom is gentle—a characteristic of God's servants.

Wisdom is willing to yield—willing to listen to reason.

Wisdom is full of mercy and good fruits—wisdom is demonstrated in word and in truth.

Wisdom is impartial—does not discriminate against others.

Wisdom is without hypocrisy—sincere and real, no play-acting.

When you pray asking God for His wisdom, He won't withhold it from you. Once you've done the asking, spend time reading His Word and listening for His Spirit to speak about your situation. It's hard for us to be quiet, but it's exactly what we need to do. Stop talking, stop thinking, and listen for the Holy Spirit. Just remember that when God speaks on a subject, it might look different from the world's answer. Refuse to allow the enemy to distract or confuse you. The enemy wants you to mull over all the options even though they are contrary to God's Word.

Therefore, the key to asking God for His wisdom is to ask in faith without doubting. James tells me if I want God's wisdom, I need not doubt He will supply. When we doubt that God will answer, we are women tossed about like crashing waves leaving us unsettled. If you decided back in Chapter One to put God first, then you can ask with confidence. Trust Him!

HEED WISE COUNSEL!

Proverbs 12:15, *"The way of a fool is right in his own eyes, but he who heeds counsel is wise."* There are times when each of us needs help. Life gets messy and often blinds us to the best direction to take while floundering in the quicksand of our struggle. When that happens, frequently people want to give us advice on how to handle our problem. Give careful thought to their suggestions since not all advice is good. Even when God uses other people to help us, we need to exercise caution before accepting counsel from our well-meaning friends. We don't need just any kind of guidance; we need Godly counsel. The best way to hear Godly counsel is by hanging out with Godly people!

You might be wondering how to spot a Godly person. Does the person walk around with a glowing halo encircling his or her head? Doubtful. However, there are some questions to consider when evaluating the person whom you plan to listen to for guidance.

1. Does their lifestyle exhibit Godly characteristics?

   Loving, joyful, kind, good, faithful, self-controlled

2. Do they follow God's principles from the Bible?

   Love God, love others, and obey the Word

3. Have they lived a life of making wise choices?

   Applying God's truths in their life decisions

4. What type of friends do they hang around?

   Friends who encourage and point others toward Jesus

5. Does their life inspire you to follow God?

   Their peace in all situations provided from God is worth pursuing

6. Do they point you to Jesus?

   They share scripture instead of their own opinion

7. Are they critical of others?

   A critical spirit is not a Godly spirit

8. Do they drag you down?

   Their life is full of sin and want you to join them in their pit

9. Are they humble?

   They acknowledge the need for wisdom from God

People who walk with God will reproduce His characteristics in their own lives. Hearing God's Word preached, praying from a humble heart, and reading the scriptures will be a priority for one who loves God. God's Will takes precedent over their own desires or will. When you observe people living out these actions, they are worth befriending. Get to know them better. Only then can you discern if they truly "walk-the-walk" or if they are pretenders. Other people influence us. Make sure those influencing you point you to God.

Never forget, God wants you to be wise and will not withhold His wisdom when you do your part. Let's recap what we've learned from this chapter.

1. We need to seek His wisdom.
2. We gain Godly wisdom through our own spiritual growth.
3. Part of Godly wisdom is our obedience to the Father.
4. Ask God for His wisdom.
5. Heed wise counsel.

This chapter touches on a few points about God's wisdom. It is by no means a complete guide to His wisdom. I challenge you to open your Bible and study it for yourself. Allow the Holy Spirit to speak into your life and guide you in your quest for Godliness. Start by reading a Proverb chapter a day for a month and see what God reveals to you. His Word is rich and valuable like rubies— grab it!

Today, I commit to read one Proverb chapter a day for a month to increase in Godly wisdom.

Date_____Signature_____

ÐIG ÐEEÞER

Chapter 5

1. In what way has Satan attacked you since you began this book?

2. What steps are you taking to gain wisdom?

3. How are you growing in spiritual matters?

4. In what area of your life do you need Godly wisdom?

5. What sin are you nurturing that's blocking your ability to gain Godly wisdom?

6. Have you allowed pride to keep you from seeking Godly council?

Chapter 6

Prayer Warriors—Attack!

The prayer chapter is at the end of my book for a reason. When you are sandwiched between putting God first and prayer, you are in the best position for the greatest results. As with any fighting regiment, you want to use your most powerful weapon. For the Christian woman, PRAYER—which causes your enemy to tremble—is your greatest defense. By now you are aware that the enemy who causes your daily battles is Satan. He has come to devastate and destroy your life. Therefore, you need to tap into the awesome power provided by God through the Holy Spirit and slay your goliaths.

There are literally thousands of books written about prayer, and you've probably read several of them. No doubt you've heard sermons or attended classes on the topic. I'm not here to disclose a new revelation on the subject, but to remind you of a few basic truths about this mighty weapon. Make no mistake, PRAYER IS WARFARE!

The definition of prayer from Merriam-Webster: 1. "an address (such as a petition) to God or a god in word or thought 2. the act or practice of praying to God or a god" Of course, as a Christian woman, I know there is only one God to whom I'm to pray, and that's the creator of the universe. Some call Him Jehovah, or Yahweh, or Lord, or Almighty, or Jesus the Christ. Our God has many names, but that's a conversation for another time. As we've discussed in this short book, God, the Father; God, the Son; and God, the Holy Spirit, is the only One who can hear and answer your prayers. Anyone who tells you differently is a deceiver of the truth.

WHY PRAY?

Since God knows your thoughts and what's in your heart, you might ask yourself, why pray? He knows what's about to roll off your tongue. What's the point? We pray, not because God doesn't know what we need, but because He desires to hear from us. It's a way of communicating with The Almighty. Remember what we talked about in Chapter one? God longs to have a relationship with his children and never grows weary of hearing from us. To nurture that bond, you have to converse.

Our best example is Jesus. Mark 1:35 says: *"Now in the morning, having risen a long while before daylight, He went out and departed to a solitary place, and there He prayed."* Here we read that Jesus got alone with His Father and prayed. Other scriptures tell us that Jesus prayed in public, before meals, for the healing of others, before making important decisions, and even to do His Father's will. Wow! He prayed about everything. If Jesus found it important to speak often with the Father about what concerned His heart, then it's important for us to do the same. Since all Christian women should aspire to be like Jesus, it makes sense to imitate His prayer life. However, following Jesus's example is not the only reason why we pray.

Hebrews 4:16 reads: *"Let us therefore come boldly to the throne of grace that we may obtain mercy and find grace to help in time of need."* We pray because we have a need or to offer up a request for someone else's need. This verse tells us that we have no reason to fear rebuke when we pray. We are to come boldly before God. No prayer is stupid—maybe misguided—but not stupid. This verse tells me I don't always receive what I deserve because God offers mercy for my past failures. Giving me more than what I deserve, He extends grace for my present needs. I'm not sure about you, but I need both in abundance.

73

Jesus said in John 14:13, *"And whatever you ask in My name, that I will do, that the Father may be glorified in the Son."* The first part of the verse tells me there's power in praying in Jesus' name. When facing hardship or stress, I need to pray with power through Jesus name. The last half of verse 13 tells me my prayer will glorify the Father. You talk to God because it brings Him glory. When you put God first in your life, you desire to talk to Him about your life—both the good and the bad. I know that some of you are control freaks. Don't try to deny it. You want to direct your life and make every decision on your own. However, when you exercise your right to pray, you come to recognize that all power and all authority is from God alone. Once you understand this principle, your humble prayers will take on new meaning. Yes, there's more to prayer than just spitting out requests.

What?
Prayer Stipulations?

Yes, there are conditions on who can pray. Gasp! Psalm 66:18 says: *"If I regard iniquity in my heart, the Lord will not hear."* Before we can even utter our prayer, we need to confess our sins so we can approach the throne of grace with a clean heart. If the Holy Spirit convicts me of a sin and I fail to admit it to the Lord, He will not hear me. I have no right to expect a "yes" answer because God won't bless my stubbornness. This verse is why it's so important to acknowledge a sin as soon as conviction stabs you. The Holy Spirit will nudge you when a sin erupts from within you. Listen to God's whisper in your ear and then confess immediately before you forget it.

Hand-in-hand with confessing my sin is harboring unforgiveness in my heart toward another person. Jesus tells me in Mark 11:25 that if I'm praying and have a grievance against another, I must offer the person forgiveness if I expect God to forgive me. This statement is hard for me. I'm a grudge holder from way back. If someone hurts one of my loved ones or close friends . . . look out . . . I'm on the warpath! Yes, I'm a minister's wife, and I wrestle with the same things you struggle to defeat. However, if I want to be a prayer warrior, I must defeat this particular sin and forgive even when the other person doesn't want my forgiveness or know he or she has offended me.

Psalms also tells me that my motives must be pure. Have you ever heard a preacher say to pray for wealth and God will make you rich? Or maybe they've told you to pray for a new car or to expect God to bless you with a high-paying job when you ask for it. Girls, if your motive is not pure, don't expect any of those things. God is not a genie in a bottle to grant wishes when we tickle His ear. He's the Almighty Father who loves blessing His children in ways that are best for them and that bring Him glory. So check your spirit before praying.

Have well-meaning people said to you that if you have enough faith, your prayers will be answered? You'll get a "yes" answer? They might even quote Jesus in Matthew 21:22: *"And whatever things you ask in prayer, believing you will receive."* All through the Bible we find that faith is an integral part of prayer. Faith reminds me that I am weak and acknowledges that God can do what I cannot. A lack of faith on my part insults God. However, the Bible also tells us that our prayers must line up with God's purpose. I can pray for years for God to heal my friend from cancer, and later God answers no. Why? I confessed my sins before praying, I had pure motives, I had forgiven those who harmed me, and I prayed having no doubt that God could heal her; yet, she died anyway. Where did I go wrong? . . . God had other plans for her. Somehow, through her death God received glory and good could come from her death. I might not ever see the why nor understand what I deemed a senseless death, but I chose to put my faith and trust in God. He knows the future and what's best for each of us.

As with any weapon, we need to know how to wield it to get the best results. In medieval days warriors practiced for years learning to use their swords to conquer their enemies. Today our military spend months and even years honing their skills with guns and other weapons of warfare to defeat their enemies. Therefore, I should be no different with my weapon of prayer.

HOW SHOULD I PRAY?

1. Pray in the powerful name of Jesus   John 14:14

2. Pray in secret   Matthew 6:6

3. Pray believing   Mark 11:24

4. Pray with an humble attitude   2 Chronicles 7:14

5. Pray without ceasing   1 Thessalonians 5:17

6. Pray with persistence   Luke 11:9-10

7. Pray fervently   James 5:16

8. Pray with thanksgiving   Philippians 4:6

9. Pray with praise on your lips   Hebrews 13:15

These are but a few of the many verses of scripture about how to pray. They are too numerous to include in this short chapter. However, I hope these get you started with your training in how to pray. Another favorite of mine is the "ACTS" acrostic that can help keep your prayers focused on all areas of prayer. Using this approach keeps me from focusing just on my requests.

- A = Adoration   Psalm 103: 1-3
- C = Confession   1 John 1:9
- T = Thanksgiving   Ephesians 5:20
- S = Supplication (requests)   Philippians 4:6

Even when we have great outlines about how to pray, where to pray, when to pray, and steps on how not to hinder prayers, there's still the haunting question: Why are certain prayers unanswered? Why is God silent? You have God's promises in His Word that He acts when His children pray. Even when we don't see immediate results, it doesn't mean God's not working on the problem. He expects us to do our part of praying until His answer comes through.

In today's world, we expect to get instant answers. Do you feel anxious or agitated when you stand in a long check-out counter line? Or how about waiting hours for your turn in a doctor's office? Often we get annoyed and think our time is wasted. We consider all kinds of things we need to accomplish while stewing in the waiting room. Even then, God has a lesson for you. Remember that when God doesn't answer your prayer request in what you deem a timely manner, you reside in God's waiting room. What's a girl to do?

Isaiah 40:31 tells me God strengthens me while I wait. *"But those who wait on the Lord shall renew their strength; they shall mount up with wings like eagles, they shall run and not be weary, they shall walk and not faint."* Don't allow an impatient attitude to wear you down. When we rush ahead of God and take matters into our own hands, we often end up defeated. Be smart and wait on God's answer; He won't let you down.

God always has a reason for the delay. He wants to teach us while we wait even when it's hard and painful. Might He be waiting until I can handle the answer? Or is He waiting until I change my heart before He changes the circumstances? Lamentations 3:25 says, *"The Lord is good to those who wait for Him, to the soul who seeks Him."* We are called upon to "hang in there" or persevere while we wait, but also to seek Him.

All authority belongs to God. We can demand nothing, but we are to ask through prayer. He is the One with all the power to answer and to change things. So stop wringing your hands in worry about a prayer request you feel is unanswered. However, it's all right to continue to remind God about it. Your persistent prayer proclaims you believe He will answer. In the meantime, be joyful—be content. God's working on it.

I asked a group of people if they would submit a short paragraph about answered prayers in their lives. Here are the results. May you receive hope for your situation and be inspired to persevere.

At 11:00 p.m. on October 23, 1980, my husband and I stopped to pick up a few groceries. Since it was close to Halloween, we thought nothing of the man wearing a ski mask—a costume no doubt—until he approached us with a gun and herded us to the back of the store. As we rushed down the aisle, this young bride prayed fervently, "Please, God, don't let him kill us; my husband's not saved yet!" I repeated my prayer until God rescued us in a mighty way. Weeks later we visited First Baptist Church of Athens, AL. Touched by their warm welcome, we continued attending. On March 2, 1981, my husband was saved and baptized by Pastor Fred Lackey. Almost forty years later, we still serve our gracious Lord and praise Him for answered prayers!

B and C Osburn

May 1, 2017, I was diagnosed with breast cancer—frightening words to hear. I prayed about the journey. God would either heal me to continue His work on earth and be an inspiration to others, or He'd take me home. Either way, I'd be healed. Through my treatments, I tried to handle them with grace so others would see God walking with me. I was blessed to have the love and support from Drew, my son, and my daughter. Three months after my last treatment, a precious friend from my Sunday school class told me her mother had been diagnosed with the same cancer as I had experienced. I was able to council her mom through each trial she would face and give her hope. This was an answer to my prayers for God to use my experience to help others. I pray for her daily as she continues her treatments. God is good—all the time! T. Owens

My friend, Betty, had a sweet baby girl late in life. Even though it was a difficult delivery with other complications, precious Misty was a blessing. Several months later Misty had run a high fever during the week. That Sunday, sitting behind Betty, I asked to hold Misty during the worship service. I noticed Misty's fever had returned with a vengeance. Once I got Betty's attention, she paled in fear. I proceeded to hold my hand up to signal Pastor Don Flippo. He stopped the service and asked me to bring Misty forward. Following James 4:14-15, the pastor anointed her with oil. He invited the congregation to lay hands upon Misty and offered a powerful prayer on her behalf. I felt her grow cool while in my arms. She fell asleep and remained fever free afterward. I'll never forget God's touching Misty.   J Garrett

My now deceased husband had been an alcoholic all of his teenage and adult life, but was in recovery when we met. We married in 1993. For the first eight years of our marriage he continued to drink often. During those years, we attended church and a weekly Bible study in a friend's home. When our small group studied James, Chapter 5 about healing, we all prayed for my husband's deliverance from alcoholism. One Wednesday night in 2001, my husband asked several men in our church to anoint him with oil and pray for him. Because he believed what God's Word said in James 5, God healed him from his alcoholism that very night. From that point on, he never craved another drink. He served God for the next five years until his death in 2006.

J. Widner

For twelve years—1992-2004—my wife's sister was estranged from the family. Often we didn't know where she resided or if she even lived until 2004. She contacted her mom and then my wife to tell them she was in poor health. At that time she wanted to reconnect and possibly come home. A month after the initial contact, my sister-in-law promised to phone our house on a Saturday. I prayed that without any prompting from me, she would recall the evening she was saved during a revival at my home church. When she called, my wife was away from the house. I answered the call and talked with my sister-in-law for over four hours. During the first hour she said she had wandered far from God, but she'd never forgotten her salvation experience. At that moment, I knew she genuinely wished to reconcile; but most of all, I knew that God had answered my prayer.   C. Garrett

Divorce—a word that strikes fear and uncertainty in a marriage. Ten years into our marriage, my husband moved to another town— alone. Around family and friends I kept up a good front for our two girls; but in reality, I was afraid and had no idea how to proceed. Each day I took the girls to school, went home, and refused to answer the phone. My life was too painful for discussion, and I didn't want anyone's advice. It was between me and God. I prayed continually, "God, please restore our marriage." When too weary to pray, I knew the Holy Spirit interceded on my behalf. Finding comfort through music, one day God gave me two hymns: "Have

Faith in God" and "My Faith Looks Up to Thee." I sang them often. The following Sunday, after taking the girls to Sunday school, I stayed for the worship service. I opened the bulletin and saw my two songs listed. God's peace settled over me. He would take care of my situation. Two weeks later my husband asked to come home. At the divorce lawyer's office a voice had spoken to him, "Do not do this!" God had answered my prayers and had begun to restore our marriage. This year we celebrated our 32nd anniversary. God is good!   Anonymous

Today I commit to fight my battles on my knees and become a mighty PRAYER WARRIOR!

Date_____Signature_____

DIG DEEPER

Chapter 6

1. Tell about a recent answered prayer in your life

2. How do you imitate Jesus' prayer life?

3. What do I mean, "there is more to prayer than spitting out requests?"

4. Who do you need to forgive so God can hear your prayers?

5. When have you used your weapon of prayer the most effectively? Give an example.

6. Are you in God's waiting room? Explain.

Chapter 7

Now What?

After working your way through this book, do you wonder if you can attain the goals you signed in each Chapter? Friend, fear not! With God's help nothing is impossible. Don't allow discouragement to cause you to do nothing. Press onward. Through my months of writing and studying to prepare for this book, the Lord convicted me of my weak areas and encouraged me in the parts I do well. I found I can't do them all well at the same time. Depending on my life struggles, my strong areas become weak and my weak areas become strong; but, it's okay. God knows I'm an imperfect girl and at times, weak—that's why I need Him desperately.

In September of this year, we received a 6:30 a.m. phone call from our son in Mississippi. Due to pregnancy complications, our daughter-in-law was about to deliver a baby girl five weeks early. Keith made arrangements with church staff to cover his responsibilities while I hurriedly packed our suitcases; then we headed to Mississippi.

Unfortunately, our sweet granddaughter had need of the NICU in a distant town while her lungs developed more fully. The following week proved stressful for all as the family made numerous trips to check on Emery. With her over an hour from home, it was emotionally difficult for our daughter-in-law who was unable to make the trip each day. Even though we knew Emery was receiving the best of care, our emotions vacillated up and down.

During Emery's NICU stay, my prayer life was on track as I persistently prayed for our little family; however, my Bible reading—nonexistent. As I helped care for the family, attended to our grandson, and made trips to Tupelo to see Emery, this weary Mimi fell into bed each night without a thought about Godly things. I couldn't concentrate to read my scriptures. You see, there are times when we are unable to practice all of God's principles at all times. He doesn't expect that either. There are occasions when unusual circumstances knock us off our sweet path. God understands. What God wants is a willing heart.

You'll be relieved to know that after eleven days in the NICU, they released Emery. She weighed 4 lbs. 3 oz. when she came home, and now at twelve weeks old she weighs 9 lbs. 5 oz. We are elated with her good progress. Our story had a happy outcome, but that's not always the case when we pray for people. However, that doesn't stop us from crying out to our Heavenly Father for His mighty Hand to heal.

Where are you today? Are you struggling with life's many battles that seem unsurmountable? Perhaps you're a single woman who wonders if God has a mate for you. You've prayed long and often for a husband, but find yourself in God's waiting room. The loneliness and frustration presses heavy against your heart. The pain is real. Or maybe you're single again because of a death or a divorce. Your anxiety and the piercing ache in your heart often seem unbearable. How are you to go forward with your life when your feet drag as if in quicksand? Will your smile ever return? Will the heaviness ever lift?

Might you be the young married woman wanting her first baby; yet, the doctors give little hope. You're praying for a miracle— possibly through in vitro or medication. Friends and family ask why you haven't started your family which only compounds your agony. Or maybe your baby was born with a medical problem that requires constant care. Pain squeezes your heart with each doctor or hospital visit. All you want is good health for the child whom you love with abandon. What about those exhausted mothers of newborn babies? Unable to form a coherent thought, they stare glassy-eyed into the darkness as they feed and rock their sweet miracle. Are you considering a job change that will move you far from family and friends or are you one who's facing financial ruin? The decisions you must make torment your every thought. Co-workers wonder at your short temper and run from your frown. The pressure from your predicament crushes the breath from your body. Your foggy brain can't hold a thought. Perhaps you're caring for an aging parent with Alzheimer's disease or another debilitating illness. You must make life altering decisions for your loved one when all you want to do is curl up and sleep away the day. How will you survive the struggle?

Any one of these life crises can take down the strongest of women and throw her off the path of her spiritual growth. You worry you're not putting God first because you are all consumed by your own tribulations. In Matthew 25:40 it tells me that when I care for one of the least in His Kingdom, I'm doing it unto Him. When I minister to others from the overflow of God's love for me, I'm putting God first. As I speak encouraging words into someone's life, I'm obeying God's Word to be kind to others. Each of us executes many of these principles as we do life. So don't stress when you get knocked off the proverbial train track of growth for a short season.

Remember—even if you apply all of God's principles to your life, there will always be battles to overcome because we live in a fallen world. However, if you start by implementing the principles in this book, they will not only help you survive, but you will also emerge a stronger person of faith.

No matter where you are on life's journey just realize that God is calling to you. He calls you to walk in His light and trust Him completely. His outstretched hand beckons you. Slip your tiny fingers into His mighty grasp, and He won't let you go. He loves you just as you are with an unconditional and never-ending love. Secure in His presence, you are prepared for any Goliath-type battle that crosses your path. You will stand firm in a world spiraling deeper into spiritual darkness and emerge fully equipped to make a difference in the moral climate in your home, our nation, and the world.

Battle on sister!

An Invitation to Know Jesus Christ

This is a matter only you can handle for yourself. You must approach God with a willing and sincere heart to know His Son, Jesus. He has been pursuing you for years.

First, you must agree with God that you are a sinner—one who has done wrong. Romans 6:23 says, *"For the wages of sin is death, but the gift of God is eternal life in Christ Jesus our Lord."* Your sins formed a deep chasm between you and God resulting in your separation from God—a spiritual death. However, at the beginning of time, God created a rescue plan through a free gift of grace.

Acts 16:31says, *". . . Believe on the Lord Jesus Christ, and you will be saved . . ."* You can do nothing to earn your way to heaven. Ephesians 2:8-9 reads, *"For by grace you have been saved through faith, and that not of yourselves; it is the gift of God, not of works, lest anyone should boast."* You must believe that Jesus died, was buried, and rose again to take away your sins—that He offers salvation as a free gift to all who believe.

Now it's time to confess. *Romans 10:9 reads, "that if you confess with your mouth the Lord Jesus and believe in your heart that God has raised Him from the dead, you will be saved."* Your prayer might sound like this:

Dear God, I know I've sinned. I realize the penalty for my sin is death. Thank you for sending Jesus to take my place. I confess and ask for your forgiveness. Today, I desire to turn from my sinful and selfish ways and receive Your free gift of grace. I accept Jesus Christ as my Savior and Lord. In Jesus precious name I pray, Amen. Welcome to the family of God!

If you prayed this prayer today and are willing, please e-mail me about your decision at authorsmsy@gmail.com.

Teresa Smyser lives in Northern Alabama with her minister husband and their deaf cat, Spock. They have two married children, one grandson and two granddaughters. She graduated from Eastern Kentucky University and now works as an accountant and divides the rest of her time between family, friends, church activities and writing. Teresa's prayer is that not only will her novels entertain, but they will point people to the love and the hope found in her Lord and Savior, Jesus Christ.

For more information about Teresa and her books, visit her at www.teresasmyser.com or www.facebook.com/teresasmyser

She loves hearing from her readers. Send questions or comments to authorsmys@gmail.com

If you found this book inspiring or helpful, please leave a review on Amazon or Goodreads. Whether short or long, your review is beneficial. Thank you again for choosing to read my books.